the dips

poems by geoff peterson
art by sharon butler

The Literature of Missing Persons
previous works by the same author

Cordes Junction (1987)
Medicine Dog (novel, 1989)
Hecho en Mexico (chapbook, 1995)
Bad Trades (novel, 2000)
Cold Reading (2007)
Crazy Stairs (2008)
Drama & Desire (2009)
The Greyhound Bardo (novel, 2009)
Cine Bahía: the *S*uicide Codex (2009)
Fiery Messengers (2010)
She Dropped Me in the Middle of Nowhere (2011)
Dark is my Therapy (2011)
Tucumcari (with Megan Collins, 2012)
The Perry Square Gospels (2012)
Penance (2013)
punto: poems with time running out (2013)
Horrible Intimacies (2014)
The Moira Cycle (2015)
Not Sleep, Deeper: on aging & living alone (2016)
No Services: 69 haiku for your driving pleasure (2017)
The Folding Chairs Meditation: prompts for a season on the skids (2017)
3:30—*nocturnes & études* (2017)
Trance States: memory, apparitions, and the movies in my gut (2018)
Archipelago: selected early poems (2019)
Death Work: the late poems (2019)
Alone, with groceries: notes on a passing world (2020)
Breakfast for Dinner: poems over easy (2020)
Open Ticket: postmortem sketches (2021)
In the Underground Garage: poems incognito (2021)
5 O'clock Shadow (stories, 2021)
False-Positive: The Quarantine Verses (2022)
The Directions to Blue Willow: out-takes & repairs (2023)
The Book of Leaving: notes, drafts & extracts (2024)

Titles available at amazon.com, barnes&noble.com or through your local bookseller.

Readers Comment on *The Dips*

Peterson's The Dips *explores universal themes of pain and remembrance, while navigating the existential crisis of our time. Sharon Butler's native faces add emotional depth both lyric and penetrating...*

—J. T. Norton
M.Ed., teacher, Honolulu

Told with poignancy and depth, The Dips *opens old wounds that never quite go away. Poems as medicine for those haunted by the feeling of not having given enough of themselves. Sharon Butler's art is an intense depiction of the solitude embedded in these poems.*

—Pam Poulsen
horse trainer / riding instructor,
Fresno, CA

In The Dips *Peterson delves into the personal dimensions we all share and that deserve our attention: the drive for self-preservation in the face of abysmal desires, the blockade of childhood trauma, and the fear of living outpaced only by the dread of death. The inclusion of the desert with its harsh light and vast expanse of emptiness is an ideal landscape for the poet's journey. Sharon Butler's artwork exquisitely compliments the poetry.*

—Karen Brandel, RN, ret.
Tucson, AZ

The "Fr. Pete" quote in The Dips *hints at the full dimension of Peterson's book. If Fr. Pete could read these poems, he'd see the ways the author has stayed alive. Peterson survives connected to friends in many places. He's faced more than his share of demons and attending angels, and has trudged a hard and beautiful journey. Enhanced by Sharon Butler's stunning desert portraits,* The Dips *is a testament to how an artist's vocation is inseparable from the man's life.*

—Andy Vinca,
Poets' Warehouse
@ Angelo's Roofing, Erie, PA

Gotham Books

30 N Gould St.
Ste. 20820, Sheridan, WY 82801
https://gothambooksinc.com/

Phone: 1 (307) 464-7800

© 2024 *Geoff Peterson*. All rights reserved.

No part of this book may be reproduced, stored in a retrieval system, or transmitted by any means without the written permission of the author.

Published by Gotham Books (June 13, 2024)

ISBN: 979-8-3302-3323-6 (P)
ISBN: 979-8-3302-3324-3 (E)

Because of the dynamic nature of the Internet, any web addresses or links contained in this book may have changed since publication and may no longer be valid.

The views expressed in this work are solely those of the author and do not necessarily reflect the views of the publisher, and the publisher hereby disclaims any responsibility for them.

This one's for Gary,
a friend who listens like a telescope
and can read the stars.

*He has also set eternity in the human heart;
yet no one can fathom what God has done from
beginning to end.*
　　　　　　　　　　　　　—Ecclesiastes 3:11

About the Title

I'd heard it first during a phone call from Jackie, an artist friend of mine. Asked how it was going, she replied, okay, but for a recent attack of the dips—to be expected. They come, they go, the usual dross coughed up from early trauma and imprinting. In her case, a voice that reminded her it's best if she not rise after a bad night to work on her latest painting.

The Dips, of course! We all had them. Before I hung up, I knew I wanted to write it. Having no idea to begin with, I launched into poems packed with age, memory, the desert, and having nothing to say; headway began to be made. I began feeling the dips in the road heading north, then south again; the dips in my bloodstream and the flow of traffic. The *dips* reminded me of the *nafs,* a word from the Sufi tradition having to do with the daily struggle with the Self, the psyche, and a pesky ego that reared its head as depression, conniving, and concupiscence. "Verily the *nafs* incites to evil," says the Quran. Dante even crept in to revive in me the vocation of a poet in the depths of Purgatory. *The Dips* would be redemptive.

Then came the visitations, mostly nameless spirits who came at night. Some would sit on the edge of my bed while I was reading. I'd feel the dip in the mattress and know who was there. One was Jack, my grandfather; another, my uncle; my mother, my father… Sometimes they'd come without a message but to merely sit beside me and share my bout with the dips. I came to understand that their presence was the message, and that mine was a comfort to them as well. Sometimes the tears came sweetly. I called my sister and asked had she ever witnessed the dips at night. Of course, she said, and we eagerly exchanged notes.

My book would begin: Supping alone from a broken bowl, what can you do when the dips come begging for seconds?

No big deal, it's just another round of the dips.

After thirty pages, I thought to consult an artist friend who draws faces, and asked to include a few from her collection. Desert faces, with eyes that don't quit. Sheets flapping on a clothesline for no other reason than it awakens the child in me. The cot in my room in a thousand motels…

Everyone's got their own tales from the dips. A whole reservoir of dips is splashed across the news every night. Dips remain secret till it's too late. This book is intended to protect our dips and soothe them into compliance. What follows is the latest dip from my dream-hoard that illustrates what I mean.

In the dream he appears in tatters, baggy trousers so threadbare it's hazardous. I suggest he go with me to a men's store and pick out some new clothes. He says let's go right now and he'll take me to dinner. Dad, I can't, I have to be alone. Instead, I'll pick you up tomorrow and we'll go to lunch. He's disappointed but agrees to my plan. But now I realize I can't do that either. I can't take the time away from my work; I've got a book to finish. I've got people counting on me to submit something by Friday. I don't know how to tell the old man. Maybe I can finesse it and be in two places at once. I've done it before. Okay then, I'll pick him up at ten and… Never mind, I can't do it, I'm too old and dammit, I'm sorry. I'll never be a son and an author in the same breath. I'll never be a person in the world and a chronicler of it at the same time. I'll never get the hang of it.

Past midnight. Switch on a light and jot down the above, then call people. No one picks up so leave a message. I'm alerting them against going forward with the book in question. It's not ready, I tell them. I've just had a dream that told me I've got to slow down and let this happen. You just can't will things to happen when each word is a decision. Let go and trust it will come to you.

Thus, once again am I rescued from the dips, and am free to devote more time to composing my life before dying. Enjoy these simple, skinny poems that I've scratched on a pad beside my bed, and perhaps you can wear one like a lost perfume while out for the evening.

Anyway, I give you *The Dips*.

geoff peterson
casa grande
2024

Table of Contents

My Tooth!	1
Danse Macabre	3
No shirt, No shoes…	5
Night Watch	6
Citizen	7
Mythos	8
Portrait of the Artist	9
Their 1st Session	10
Business as Usual	11
Another Story	12
Love Seat	14
Gifted, Beautiful	16
Check List	17
On Death Row	18
Evaluating the Veteran	19
Joe Luckey	20
What the Market Bears	22
Natural Causes	23
Test Drive	24
The House of Sleep	25
Sonora	26
What I'd Tell Him	27
At the Old Piedmont	28
Last Night's Dream	29
Ghost Songs	30
Owl Song	32
Serving Life	33
TV Fare	34
The Girl Can Write	35
Phantom Dog	36

Sports Book	37
Monument Valley	39
Her Nibs	40
Treacherous Traffic	41
Attention, Seniors	42
Vertigo	43
The Fine Print	44
Everyone's Got a System	45
White Rooms	47
My Visitor	48
Dave, Shaving	49
Routes 39, 54	51
Fill-Up in Dalhart	52
Jack's Last Days	54
Senior Matinee	55
Irish Jim	57
The New Grand	59
Hotel Carl	61
Reconnaissance	62
Namesake	64
Summer Solstice	65
Reading the Cards	66
The Dips	67
The Ache	69
Good Friday	72
Last Call at The Golden West	74
Say It	75
Uncle, at the End	77
Just In Case	78
In the Path of Totality	79
Epithelium	80
Anywhere	81

Proving Grounds	82
Interstate Motel	83
At French Creek	84
Desert Song	85
The Interview	86
Movies We Showed That Winter	88
Rosie's Motel	89
The Road Out	91

My Tooth!

Emotions ran high
that Saturday in Pennsylvania.
As announced: Billy Kearns' sister's engagement
to a Marine with gold buttons…
date set for May.

I wanted to scream *don't do it! the biggest mistake*
a girl like Marjorie can make.
Wait for me!
      I was Billy's friend
and more in love with Marjorie than I could suffer.
She worked nights at the phone company
and took breaks in the back room,
eating an egg sandwich.
I think she's dead now.

Billy was a bully and gained weight in ways
that gave his mother fits.
But for now he'd sit on my chest and tickle till I'd
      fart
and break into tears.

Marjorie was eighteen and busy with her hair,
but she made Billy pin me while she bent down
and kissed me on the lips!
      I cringed, I must've,
and lay wracked with shame.
My tooth, my tooth! I cried
and rushed home not stopping once
to look both ways.

In my room not knowing what to do,
I pretended to die, to go through it
and come out the other side where all that
had floated away.
      And when I relaxed
I rose from bed,
went to the window
and touched my lips in awe.

Danse Macabre

A love like that was a serious illness, an illness from which you never entirely recover. —Charles Bukowski

Some days felt like
being in a movie with Gloria
Graham wearing nothing
but a mink coat with pockets
deep enough for a gun.

Let it be my turn
to open a vein and admit
the God-awful truth
without alcohol.

Ten years lying to ourselves,
has it not? It's been swell,
adieu, we said finally,
taking the elevator.

But as the man in the bar
advised: you can't expect
living with somebody
to feel the same as
living alone.

Now what say we drop
this charade and hop
the next flight and
I will meet you.

We'll drive somewhere
in a car we'd never
afford to own—

then book a room
and make ourselves hungry.
We'll order the special
and sit on the terrace
before closing.

And you'll recall
stepping off the plane and saying
I can do this!

No shirt, No shoes...

I'd begun to stutter
in memory of my uncle
who thumbed west in search
of work and ordered
ham & eggs at a diner—
then opened the paper
to Sports to see
how his team was doing.

Having come so far
to catch a break, just to find
nothing… Here, it's on
the house, said a waitress
named Blanche.

Later I'd find myself
in downtown Los Angeles
and walk my restless phantoms
in honor of St. Roch,
patron saint of dogs and
bachelors with filthy habits.

```
Night Watch
```

The room a monk's cell:
cot, chair, crucifix…
A light from the alley
cuts like a scythe and
trembles in corners.
I savor these moments—
a boy in my uncle's bed,
waiting for him to cough,
crush his cigarette and
roll against the wall.
He smells of beer
from Milwaukee and says
he saw the girl I like
with her sister at
a bowling alley
talking to another boy.

```
Citizen
```

Being of sound mind
and a hermit in good standing,
I accept the lessons
of history and the collapse
of empires in the wake
of civil unrest...

Fact-checked to death,
anything said can be used
against me.

Meditations
on the corrupt body,
the nonsense of this world...
What can a man do
when the dips pull up
at a highway motel
and insist on talking
back to the TV?

We're all cruising
these soft-spoken nights
through Hell or Purgatory.
If Dante hadn't been
blind-sided by that
interview with the Pope
the *Commedia* would've
never happened.

Mythos

Ancient legends of heroes
teach us our wounds
are foretold in the trauma
at birth—the secret
of being: a new found
state of forgetfulness
as destined to sculpt
one's character.
I am trying to say
something unspeakable.
Witness my own scathing.

Portrait of the Artist

A besotted green sweatshirt,
frayed, paint-globbed and
inside-out...

"ill-fitting blue trousers"
his work clothes during the war years,
describing Picasso.

My father's blue pajamas
worn through with good intentions
and devotion to silence.

No rings, no watch, but
unmatched socks with holes—
used for handkerchiefs.

He was a good man, my father,
ensconced in the tabernacle
of his staggering loss.

So I wear them,
splotched and pee-stained—
and toss in the hamper.

Their 1st Session

As she applied pressure to the sole
of his right foot, he pointed out
the very spot, it's been said,
that if touched just so
with the right amount of pressure,
it would induce such weeping
that it might never stop.
And she said for best results
better that he not speak
during treatment.
Of course, he said,
and for the rest of the hour
struggled to keep from farting.

Business as Usual

Zombies captured on tape
via security cameras,
suffering from PTSD
or post-apocalypsis,
staring into phones while
waiting at check-out…
My life is broken
or I'd leave and
start anew.

Another Story

I think all night on my back
and wake exhausted.
My idea of a made bed—
the album jacket for
Slaughter on 10th Avenue
when vinyl was cheap
and I'd only just begun
suspecting grownups…
but that's another story.
Thus I write this
on doctor's orders,
this is it: one life,
one comma, the last dotted i.
If having nothing to say
would only stop it.

Love Seat

But Purgatory is a mother quest...
                —*Harriet Rubin*

Mother, is that you?
My bed, see there—
it dips!

The prophecy in blood,
fulfilled— *finally,*
drawn to his despair,
she will appear again
in his room and
hear his breath
stop:
    Look,
she comes back
and wants to tell me!

Tell me where you come from,
how you got here and
what happened.

Stay with me and
hum the tune you loved.
See, a ¾ moon rocks
in the bare branches.

Silence is a kingdom.

Alone, you taught me
a man weeps for the souls
in Purgatory, and yearns

for a single drop
of sweetness.

Rest now, my prince.
So many poems
and so little coffee…
And to think all we meant
to each other merely
a splash of light.

Gifted, Beautiful

That summer I saw his obit in the paper—
an old friend's older brother,
dead at seventy.

Natural causes, it said,
but we who'd moved away,
married, divorced, cut on
and opened by surgeons
knew the score.

The shy but gifted one
drank in secret and
lived in a convent,
a groundskeeper who
ran errands for the nuns.

I hadn't seen them since
my friend lost his scholarship,
married and took a job
in finance, while his brother
stayed and studied chess.

But my friend had aged
and drove up from Baja—
top down, for the funeral,
baffled by what came before
or what comes after.

Check List

*Rather than discuss the merits of your writing,
let's talk about what you do to stay alive.*
                              —Father Pete

Stretch...make bed...record dreams...
    take pills...make coffee...

brush teeth...feed birds...sweep up droppings...
check messages...cancel appnts...walk outside...
    dispose of mail...

yogurt, fruit...laxative...pray...light the candle...
    read Thought for Today...

dust...work on revisions...look up *sacerdotal*...
count quarters for laundry...take a bath...play
a loose game of solitaire...

exercise hands...dust...make coffee...
    read Kotaro's *Chieko Poems*...
        look up *Seitosha.*

tune in baseball...count pills...drink water...
empty garbage...dust...consider a life...
heat a pot pie, bean soup...
    check my revisions...
change back to the way they were...

p.s. find the photo of myself as a boy—
    just before the crash.
    There he is, I got it now.

On Death Row

My uncle talking
without pause or stammer…
*Think of it as the first time
you got laid,* he says,
speaking of the unquenchable.

That time in his car after
grilling hot dogs for a dollar —
not enough to buy a condom
with a girl whose voice
embarrassed him.

Marriage by shotgun
and the promise of a job
to feel grown up,
being severed from the Air Force
with a nerve disorder.

Love, desire…
the difference being one's sense
of heaven, one's glimpse
of what's ahead and
it's not scary.

Still hesitant to make
his point clear, he comes
in stealth, an aspect
of myself I hardly knew
but have not relinquished.

Evaluating the Veteran

He struggled last year,
but knows what he's doing—
he's been around.
Got a 86-90 mph heater,
a tricky curve, a cutter,
a sinker, a splitter
and a slider that's his
bread & butter…
Sometimes he gets beat up,
but hey, the doc says
his elbow's shot but his instincts:
right down the middle!
He'll eat up innings for you
as a middle reliever, and
he'll take a pay cut.

Joe Luckey

In fact, he wasn't, if by luck you mean things
come sweetly when you least expect.
       Witnessing a man's life
instructs in ways words are made for.
Call it eulogy.

I wasn't old enough to know
he'd studied to be a priest,
but the Latin and those
pesky declensions
tend to stymie.

While failing three times
despite the help of tutors, one learns
you don't get what you want
being stubborn.

Joe got on with Maintenance
loading boxes, but rose to
head janitor and
stayed his entire
shift on earth.

Faculty came and went,
students matriculated in waves,
I left home, roamed about,
returned and took classes.
Joe remained.

Unmarried and without honors,
he'd been born already old:
bald, squat, bent over,

keys clanging that opened
underground doors…

In his last years he joined
a theatre organ society,
attending conferences
in musicology and
the legacy of forms.

Once inviting me
to his basement apartment,
he unveiled an entire church organ
in pieces—in carefully marked boxes.

He kept things pristine, inviolate—
instruments that forbade touching,
as required for sanctity.

Decades later I'd visit the dead
in their habitats and enter
their hidden portals…
and there, beside the statue,
a tree-lined alley named
Joe Luckey Way.

What the Market Bears

The callers keep calling,
urging that you enter your latest
in an "International Book Fair"—
coming soon.

Berlin, Miami, *Los Angeles Times*,
each with slots waiting…
Will run you a thousand, not including
travel, hotel, meals & tips.

But think of the advantages in meeting writers
just like yourself. Trust me, it's time
you get on board with this—
really!

Wait a minute. Now tell me,
why would I want to meet
anyone like myself?

It hurts to say this but
I'm fifteen years older than Hemingway
the morning he pushed two shells into a 12-gauge
and then into his head.

When you're lured into the spotlight
called yourself, you play the fool,
said somebody.

And the biggest upside to being nobody
is knowing who you are.

```
Natural Causes
```

Some days it burns,
or it's a drunken friend who won't shut up.
I put him in the car, buckle him in back
and ask if he's comfortable.
He tells me I'm doing this
all wrong.

He tells me of his dread of being sick
and unable to find a place
without insurance.

So I drive around cutting deals in the rear view.
He'll stop taking his pills like my buddy
and we'll drive out into remote lands
and sit in my car to wait.

Clean, quiet, dust swept up in drafts…
They'll say he was working on
a book when he died.

```
Test Drive
```

So we test a Jag convertible
and load it with copies of
my book and aim it like
a bullet at the heart
of Hollywood and
pitch it to studios
as *film noir*, shot on the cheap
with fog, rain, and a guy
who resolves to not beat up
his girlfriend again.
*A tender love story that veers
off course*, says the clip.
Starring ourselves, of course,
back from retirement,
and introducing newcomer
Jessica Darling
as herself.

The House of Sleep

You remember lying out
on the moonlit mesa,
waiting to be found
and airlifted to the stars.

Watching your belly burst
from festering, the flesh baked
with festive black ants…
Where is my life now,
and what's happened to me?

Having drifted too far,
you lose where this started…
where you are, what happened
and why it should matter
to no one in particular.

Sonora

This the sunlit pool
Margot entered
and introduced
grackles to me
which I'd mistaken
for crows, and
each desert plant
in bloom, named,
as well the endless sky
we lay in when
I loved her.
It was almost like
knowing the truth
about yourself and
what happens that's
unforeseen and
not once thinking to ask
the woman to stay.

What I'd Tell Him

Kid, you're here on purpose—
visiting from another life
going on elsewhere
as we speak.

With much unfinished business,
you'll meet a spectacular death
and return to the sorceress
you were—in exile.

There aren't words
for what we walk through,
only the next blind step
and the next…

the breath going out of us.

At the Old Piedmont

That year in Oakland
my kid and I were friends
and met for matinees.
She sold candy, popcorn
from behind a counter
and wore a uniform.
I'd sit in the mezzanine
among regulars with
shopping bags, chocolate
or snoring, each of us
lost in a motion picture
of his own making…
Just thinking of it
feels like waking up
to the music that swells
just before the end.

Last Night's Dream

I overheard my ex-wife
reading my old story
to a friend over the phone—
a speaker phone so I can
hear her comments.
Often she'd interrupt
until my ex instructed that
she keep her comments
to herself until there's
a break in the story—
a rest, as it were.

My wife read the dialogue
in voices appropriate
to each, and even added
sound effects…
I was so flattered it
woke me up.
The wind was blowing
the shade away
from the window…
when it stopped
and I rose to start the coffee.

Ghost Songs

Solace of trees
on the windswept terraces
sparkling in the night…

Twitching on the floor
after working, my tongue
a lump of dust…

Since I've lost hearing
I listen to hear it:
the whistling stream of souls.

No need to call a doctor.
Weak and herniated,
let me count the minutes.

One more day
of pipes bursting or rats
gnawing under the hood…

I long to find
the places our parents
found to be alone.

Do not read further
unless you're comfortable
driving after dark.

The dead don't have
the answers and refuse
to hire a service.

Driving now, tell them
it's best you go home
as some desires go unmet.

If you hear from anyone
I know, don't tell them
where I am.

```
Owl Song
```

See yourself snatch
at pieces to get through it.
Lounge lights to soften
the storm, you sleep
in parking lots and find
not one untamed thing
worth leaving.
Such is the night
you've been selected
to return to.

Serving Life

For the remission of sins
and settling old scores,
our children have stashed us
in retirement homes,
unfit for service
since we voted Republican
and drove the car when
it was forbidden.
In the evening I'll listen
to Pound in my room
read *The Cantos*—
recorded in an asylum
a mad century ago.
Aiuto: help, the last
word of the last poem
mumbled in his cell.
Show me a man without
enemies, I'll show you
a man without.

TV Fare

I'd get a movie channel
with my rabbit ears
and a tuner box.
I'd get *films noir*
and a slew of westerns
from the Forties.
Jack likes a good western
when it suits him.
Pull up a chair.

On Sundays foreign flicks
where the director knew
what he was doing and
did it anyway.
Next a reality show
where a bouncer assists
disgruntled customers
off the premises—
have a nice day!—
when I catch sight of
an old girlfriend
on a Viagra commercial.
Jack says whatever the hell
I see in this shit
escapes him.

The Girl Can Write

There's a book I'm reading
I can't put down and stop
at a very early stage
to look her up to make
sure she's real and
eats meat.

Even her characters
are clothed in tenderness
run to ground.
I would reach out and
propose marriage,
but that would mean
moving to New Jersey.

Which gets me thinking:
there isn't much I'd trade
for love, and must say
I never have, *boo-hoo!*
As Kerouac would say:
Put that in your Broadway show!

Phantom Dog

Walking the beast at dusk,
I pay attention to a swarm
of small things...

*(notice how
hair settles and
collects in corners.
Mother would go nuts:
    sigh)*

while teaching my furry friend
how to find his way home
without me.

Sports Book

Ham 'n egg-ers hunch
over game sheets with
pencil stubs while
bifocals ride their noses…
An air-cooled largesse
installed to titillate, satiate,
but never satisfy.
Gazing at walls of ballgames,
races and leader boards,
I hear my grandfather
urge me to stop
what I'm doing and
finish a rabid cup of coffee.
Don't end your life
a lonely man, he says
after scanning yesterday's
results from Hialeah.

Monument Valley

For one solar hour
clocked with shadows
on the cliff's face,
recalling the years I learned
the art of shedding skin
to acquire new ones and
refresh myself.
The rage to recycle:
a new home, pleasant
spouse—roots put down
somewhere else…
While all that time,
death was a monument
to a life in the sky.

Her Nibs

Be it resolved,
I will not permit my ex
to kill me. I said it
then, I say it now—
to all the others
who spend their lives
training to become
assassins-in-waiting.

Treacherous Traffic

Driving for hours
readies you for the next
breakdown without battery,
phone or flashlight—
where lovers are chill
and death a sloughed off thing.
Only the spirits of native
chiefs can suppress
your grosser handicaps.
Love, grief, hardship…
ablutions of the heart—
an outer region where
even firewater fails.
Unrepentant, you'll never be
as you were again.

Attention, Seniors

Waking up without earplugs,
I search for the pair that
fell out last night.
Not for music or books-
on-tape but pods to keep
the dips out.

If it comes from above
or below, I can't say
but suspect by dips
I mean the syncopated solo
in my lizard brain.

A friend suggests white noise—
relying on her CPAP
to work hers out.
I'll try it because I'm old
and there might be others
haunted by the dips
in *their* heads.

You see, I am among those
left to help each other
through sorrow, but
otherwise seclude.

```
Vertigo
```

Pain, breathless,
too weak to walk,
and done pretending,
I tell myself that
checking off chores
on my calendar
will save me.
Drowning in the hours
without desire
is my hell.

The Fine Print

Grandfather comes
overdressed for the heat
to hear me go on about
the nuisance of ads
in today's mail:
credit card gimmicks,
subscription discounts
for a limited time only…
miracle drugs that
make you jittery…
memberships
promising wellness or
a chance to get lucky,
but leave you the same
as before…

Grandfather waits
for me to calm down:
cigarette, a sip of coffee.
Read the fine print, he says.
Think how the Apaches felt
dealing with settlers
back in the day.
      Now,
read me the menu, will you?

Everyone's Got a System

Mine's counting the days
backwards to my birth,
totaling 28 thousand
& change, including
leap years.

Meanwhile I'll count
groceries, money,
the gallons of gas
burned to get me
to the next traffic stop…

*Just get me through this,
Officer, I'll be fine.*

White Rooms

Walls pocked with holes
from portraits and certificates
of completion…

Microwave'd cup of soup,
a shower without curtain and
a toilet named Giselle.

Unsalted nuts, coffee crystals,
and watching a western…
Air courtesy of a unit that
bangs all night and
smothers the patter
of busy mice.

Dining at the café
in a corner booth
is Magdalena.
Mother of two,
she keeps me
tuned to her saga:
a boy in pre-school,
troublesome but
innocent of passion.

A vision to behold,
and I dare say—
friendly in a strange
disarming way. But—
I've been thinking,
and it's okay having all that
over and done with,
behind me.

My Visitor

Residence at the Starlight Motel,
room 808 next to
the ice machine…

on Pioneer Blvd.
across from State Line Café,
Nowhere Nevada.

Just getting by
on savings and a monthly check.
Cash rolled in a microwave.

The mind's an open window
filled with sky and
nature's morphine.

I don't gamble and don't
play golf. I walk, read,
follow the leader board
between naps…

Now the wind swells
and rattles the door…
Jack, is that you?

He wants to know if
he can borrow some money,
he's got a game going next door.

Dave, Shaving

All civilizations are doomed.
—Guido Cavalcanti

Drawing blood, he dabs
with toilet paper. Where were we?
We're all dying, I said:
you, me, civilization,
the collected worlds
of Lord Shiva…

Drip…drip…
in the steamy mirror.
Who will stop the bleeding?

Dave, let us retire
to a rented room and
cogitate. I'll lie down
with my coffee and
listen to radio shows
warmed over from youth.

And you, Uncle,
clean shaven and dressed
for burial. Tell me
what has really changed
that we haven't made happen
to ourselves?

Routes 39, 54

The dips in the road
from Tucumcari north
lull you to sleep with
the hum of summer love,
hauling furniture to make her
house complete, yourself
a piece from the past.

At night before curling in back
to the hum of crickets and
dreaming of pancakes tomorrow,
you'll walk among bungalows
and cars on blocks…

Didn't they tell you
the dips will convene to say
all there is to go by?
That you love this country
but cannot go on for
another haunted mile?
Turn around instead
and seek the palace
unmet in memory.

Fill-Up in Dalhart

Nobody goes there,
unless sporting Texas plates and going home
to see the missus.

Life has crashed, you see,
and we're all looking to stop the drill—
only we don't know it.

But I was just passing through.

Shaded, neat, tucked in,
grass freshly trimmed and swept to the curb...
trees shimmering like movie queens.

A dream of every day being the same.

So I chug into this 76 station on my last fumes,
show the girl a credit card, step outside
and commence to fill.

The thing about stepping into a dream—
you forget who's dreaming,
everything so calm.

Calm enough to fill up, pour a cup,
and pay at the counter.

This was back in the day you'd fill up
for under thirty dollars. Throw in a pack
of smokes and a beer that quenches...

I'm settling up when I see it—
the point of this whole encounter:
the cashier.

A high school kid with a summer job,
and knocked up by a boyfriend from the rigs,
I'd bet. Blond, lean, soft-spoken,
as calm as a sleepwalker…

Take me away from here, she says with her eyes.
Wherever you're going, take me there.
I am loved, but it's not enough.

I pulled away from that place without a word,
afraid to look back. Until now.

Jack's Last Days

I can almost hear
the ballgame on radio
and smell the liniment
on his sore back.
Upstairs in bed
with paperbacks, coffee,
a carton of Raleighs,
and reading Max Brand
or Zane Grey...
He liked westerns
and even wrote some
before the cancer made
his lungs spongy...
Like Doc Holiday in the pulps,
with no insurance to cover
his burial... All my life
nearly an exact copy.
I rode with the stranger
across the river and
smelled the purple sage!

Senior Matinee

I can't tell you how it does my heart
good to see so many turn out
for *Nightmare Alley*,
the original.

We found the last two seats
in the dark, when I asked
did she not think Tyrone Power
the most tragic figure
ever, and she said
"Pu-lease."

It broke his heart
having to convince Zanuck
he must prove himself
a true actor and thereby
change his life
or die—which he did
after the pictured flopped.

At today's special showing,
I'll count the close-ups
of the wreckage
and lounge in its awesome
waywardness.

We suffer to love ourselves
and our people on earth,
and once healed, can begin
to love each other—
broken, hell-bent,

destroyed…
hopeless of a way out.

I hereby resolve to take
Joan Blondell into the custody
of my heart, and whisper
there now, it's all right,
you're with me now.

Irish Jim

Don't say you never saw your name
in lights, he said, unveiling a sign
announcing *Reading Tonite*
by yours truly.

He thought it a hoot to hang it
in neon like a goddamn
Broadway show.
My first book in real life—
in hardback, no less, and
stacked in the lobby.
You're a celebrity!
Jim even managed to squeeze
a buck from the department to cover
my room at the hotel.

That night signing copies I pretended
to read each student's future
and make a prediction:
You will encounter problems…
and one may kill you.

At breakfast Jim gave me
my plane ticket and asked what's next?
It's scary, I said, like gazing into
a murky crystal ball.

So he reminds me: *you know,*
you don't have to go. You
don't have to go back,
if you don't want.

But I'd go back, all right.
I had family and a job that
kept me from my work
but was good for me.
In fact, I had to get back
first thing tomorrow and…
God, I'm so tired,
help me know what to do.

The New Grand
[Rock Springs, Wyoming]

As sure as God made crossroads and talk radio,
the New Grand's become a habit.
Inserted between Christ Ministries
and the pool hall, and across from
OK Bar and Kenpo Karate,
a sign says help wanted.

Inside is post office green
with pink counters and booths raked
beneath a pagoda canopy.
Good luck scrawled in Chinese
and a bowling trophy.

The jukebox plays everything
from the ridiculous to the sublime.
And there's no such thing as
private conversation,
all politicians being the same.

A waitress named Blanche lives upstairs
with a box TV and photos of a son
deployed with the Marines.
She works all day and counts
receipts at closing.

The menu runs three pages longer than
the phone book, and a sign lists
mileage to bad places…

Blanche says it don't matter
if you've been, this is where
the asphalt ends and the West begins.
This its Green Room, its Green River
and want-ads, dime tips & Lucky Strikes,
wrecked cars and phony IDs…

And the music of our lives
rains down where we lift our cups
and wait for a bus that doesn't come.

Hotel Carl

how I love to recall
the old wino twist
the cap off a pint
of Gypsy Rose

in a room upstairs,
his boxcar fingers take
care to unscrew
and not spill a drop

God loves us so much
to make a man's
first swallow
holy

Reconnaissance

Maggie being a senior, you were new
and gave her History notes after
she'd flunked it and forced to repeat.
       She'd call to tell you
where she babysat, so you'd walk there
and rock on a child's swing, waiting
while the parents looked for keys
and left a number.

Maggie would bet you're good at Math,
being a boy who wore glasses.
So you faked it till you couldn't
and recounted the French adventure
in Indo-China instead.
       Dien Bein Phu
reckoned a tactical blunder,
not to mention the boldness of the Vietminh.
Thus her bra loosened, and alas,
her panties said Friday.

But some mistakes, they said,
a boy didn't come back from:
the Gulf of Tonkin that year
a harbinger of things to come.
And this girl, this senior,
wanted you.

But girls made you nervous. You never knew
what to say, didn't own a car or carry
a Pennsylvania license...
didn't play sports, didn't have
a weekend job or money...

Didn't go to parties or to games
or rallies...ate lunch alone
and hid behind the door
of your locker.

But this girl, this senior,
wanted you.

Remember her clinging
when you stood to leave, jeans bursting and
her body urging you downward?
You walked home asking how you'd read
so many books, yet remained
so blind and stupid.

You were sure to be among those
listed as missing or lost.

Namesake

I was 10 when introduced to the wife
of my father's friend who inquired
which name I preferred to go by,
my legal name or the one
Father called me. I said
I didn't know, either
was okay, I guess.

She said it must be exciting to be
a young man unsure of
whether to live in this world
or the next.

I could not imagine what
that meant, but if she meant
what I thought it did—
Madam, please,
spare me the grief.

Summer Solstice

In the day's late heat
I decide to work nights
and go for walks
at dawn.

Maybe I'll get to stay up
late like I used to,
listening to grown-ups,

or watch late-night TV,
or maybe hit a run
of luck at poker
and play till dawn.

Either way,
my grandfather smiles
and says get some sleep.

Reading the Cards

In today's edition the man leaped
from the 9th floor of our hotel,
a martyr or fool, they argue,
all styles considered.

Evil strictly a human thing,
no wonder they call this
a vale of tears and
bear it forward.

I asked Margot to consult
the hermeneutics before
dealing her cards.
Avoid tall windows, she says.

In love, abandon hope
in crossing over, coming back.
If too old to keep appointments,
weigh your options.

The Dips

Slim shows up with a bad case of them...and says he's got to lie prone to make sense of things.

I prescribe a return to his place on earth—where it's early and no one's up... He'll walk the streets looking into windows and catch himself looking....

When he sees it: he's old and it's him.

We enter a tunnel beneath the tracks that divide downtown and come out at a hotel and a café barely open.

And who's there but Lola, renewed...like she'd died and risen. Taking her in my arms I squeeze to find she's real... and announce I'm here at last, so let us go forth and delight in each other.

Lola, a Gemini, speaks from experience and often shrewdly, smiles sadly and says what about the one inside you... the one who says staying is just a bad accident waiting to happen, who insists you move on? You always do.

Food for thought, she said. I tell her if she'll teach me, I'll listen, but that I'm fearful of beauty in all its forms will ravish.

She reminds me that she's with someone else who's good for her...it's with him she's found the best way she knows how to live.

I've released my hold on Lola since it's unseemly… I don't know who I am or where I'm headed… It takes Slim, a friend, to help me to a doctor.

After we leave, he says I'll be all right, I'm just paying dues for being who I am, that's all.

The Ache

You, our IUD baby—
that's the strain you endured
becoming a person.

It's always the unwanted
who grows to become
pharaoh.

Born with defects, you were
incubated and not
allowed to be held
but for feeding.

Your mother enrolled you
at the Y's infant care
so she could work.
She liked Arabian horses
and my salary alone
not enough.

I miss Mom, you'd cry,
riding in the car with bottled
breast milk, and only found
solace in a retractable pen
from my pocket.

The day you announced
you would grow up to be
a paleontologist or
a gym teacher…

The day I left
your mother, you flew apart
and hugged my ankles:
Dad, don't go!

On the children's ward
you grasped the doctor's hand
and walked down the hall
to surgery.

Who could say then
it would be your calling?
So much wreckage
lay beneath the surface
and would yet have to happen.

Good Friday

The Lord's Prayer—
twice as long in Spanish:
I thought you should know.

Rich black hair
and red bows for the girls,
mantillas for the mothers...

The utter cadence
of children in rows with grown-ups...
little ones taken to the toilet
during prayers by
a big sister...

the chiseled Savior
upon a rough-hewn cross,
knelt before and kissed
by patient mourners...

each assigned a role
performed in procession
for this passion,
each knowing what's expected.

Buried in the heart
of every public worship—
a private prayer:
*I am alone. Come to me
and sit on the bed.*

Last Call at The Golden West

Cookie, it's been
how many years—eleven, twelve?
As old now as you were then,
I'm every bit as weary.
My hearing aid's broke
again, so I'll nod yes
to the waitress and
get something on toast
I never ordered.
I miss that time
at this same table
we ordered the works
and raised hell, remember?
Now it's quiet but for a few
roughnecks at the bar.
The places we loved
go on without us, you said.
It's lonesome now, sitting here,
talking to a chair.

Say It

My sister being with her
at the end tells it
this way:

Confined to bed at home
whispering the rosary,
her pain constant…

"If I could only move
my bowels," she prayed,
this woman my 2nd mother.

A wise man lives
many separate lives
in a lifetime, goes the adage.

Father unable to say it,
my sister had to tell her:
Mom, it's cancer.

I'm sorry, it's eaten up
everything inside.
Cancer will do that.

The woman knew the truth,
her mind sharp, but still
someone had to say it.

Say it, she said.
I'm dying, it's okay.
I'm ready now.

Uncle, at the End

It's been seventeen years
since I began to
outlive you.
Am I ready now to
consider your life's
final stages?
Seventeen years since
you dropped the phone
watching TV and
I flew out to see
what happened and
how our lives
snap in a heartbeat.

Moved to Intensive Care,
propped upright and
lashed to a bed,
wires sprouting like hair…
monitors, circuits
meant to keep one
alive in limbo,
they made you into
something monstrous.
Pull the plug, we said,
and were given each
some time alone
with the truth
of remaining alive
alone on earth.

Just In Case

You were wondering
what remains of me
in the desert after
eleven years…

Two words: *the sky,*
meaning everywhere,
and by that I mean
all things as one.

I'll head elsewhere
to get my heart broken,
but I always come back
to feel it.

Nothing holds
a man's attention like
a herd of thunderheads
roaring through the canyon.

In the Path of Totality

Birds, ravenous, they say.
Watch them.

Remind my friend
to watch her nervous dogs
alert to disturbances.

How the limbs of trees
teach me more than books,
I've noticed.

You could say I am coming
into my own.

Glasses to watch
the Apocalypse with,
for $9.99 if you call
right now.

Afterwards we wept
and cooled our eyes in the dark.

Relieved of our dips,
we said let's go somewhere
and seek the last shadow standing.

Epithelium

*When you finally manage to utter
what you wish to utter,
the rest is silence.*
    —Dante Alighieri

Time is short
by the internal clock
in your guts, so work
till nothing's left,
not one breathless line
left in the pouch.
Over, done.

What is unveiled
engraved in the heart,
and sleep regarded only
a dream laboratory.
Step now into a life
beyond reality and
the hours of perpetual dips.

A woman's touched
your hand and whispers:
*Sometimes there's snow
on the mountain and
wildflowers...*
and urges that you
embrace this shining hour.

Anywhere

Open to nameless spaces
the air roars then claps
the sky shut, and the light
settles like furniture.
Check yourself
if that's you having
another of your episodes
or a sign of impending doom.
Now walk to the car
and recall what it takes
to drive anywhere,
and what the point of all that
was anyway.

Proving Grounds

You tried that morning
in the huge bed at
Mickey's Feldspar Spa
& Driving Range...
but she was famished,
so you got breakfast
at the casino and drove
north in a rented car
when she touched you
and brought the conversation
to a halt.
    Coitus interruptus
in the back seat, you kept
having to stop to see
if you were being
encroached upon by
cops, bikers or aliens from
Alpha Centauri.

And she, a Buddhist nun,
warned you against
hungry ghosts like
ex-wives and partners
who'd cheated you
in that nasty business.
Don't stop, she said,
hugging what she wanted,
which was you inside her
at the center of all that
emptiness at the edge
of this world.

Interstate Motel

When you consider
the chances of minor outage
in a man's brain inhibitors
could lead to mass murder,
the call for human modification
becomes urgent,
says the TV.

Scared of each other,
and too many to keep fixed
on the rails, we become suspects
and succumb to the soft
violence of authority—
social scientists,
diplomats at Davos,
herd psychologists
and the media lackeys…

Humans will run, hide, or
mingle with a robot population.
Some will resort to desolate
places and bump into
night stalkers,
their smartphones blinking
in an empty lot.

Note the frazzled stare
nailed to the motel mirror,
the creep of dementia
through shredded arteries,
the floor covered with glass
while the rats binge on
take-out cartons.

At French Creek

So many moons ago
I slipped into the shallows
beneath this bridge
and settled in mud.
Cardinals, blue jays,
black birds with
shiny green bellies...
Baptized downstream
early into a strange life,
taught by my father to swim
and to help my mother die.
I love you. I always have.
Writing this wet, my hand
makes the words bleed
and the page wrinkle.

Desert Song

It feels like you died
and just hanging around.
Tedium so deep it becomes
death's sweat lodge.
Now spend these
remaining hours
watching smoke rise
from burning mesquite.
Regardless of how,
you'll stand at the brink
of something less familiar.
A man in slow motion
cannot be jarred loose
from his shadow
till the light vanishes.
How long it's been
since you've last wept
bothers you, so turn
to what was before
not there, and resolve
to forget who you were
or what was hoped you'd become.

```
The Interview
```

In the dream an angel comes
to tell me my call was
discussed...

and it's been decided that
I will depart just as I'd
requested...

but would come back
straightaway in a foreign body,
born to a mother who's—
for lack of a better word—
distracted...

I'll be raised by agents
responsible to the government,
and as a young woman
I'll be hired to coach
a team of troubled youth.

(here I'm shown
by way of preview
my astonishment
at our first day's practice).

But there's a catch, I'm told.
I will retain all memory
of this life while
living in the next.
Such will be
my burden

for having used the past
to my advantage.

And I wept bitter tears
that robbed me of breath,
for I saw the cost of memory
to an old man and was
horrified.

Movies We Showed That Winter

Hitchcock's *Notorious* for starters…
John Ford's *Grapes of Wrath* that
drew students assigned to write
a paper for school without
having to read the book.
At William Wyler's
The Best Years of Our Lives,
they even clapped!
      For Halloween,
a special viewing of *The Mummy*
with Boris Karloff waking
one eye at a time
in an ancient chamber.
We even invited a professor
of Archaeology to come
and tell us his work
was sadly different.

Mike managed the projector
while Linda his wife
made popcorn & coffee.
I'd supply the videos
and handouts dishing
 the dirt on the stars,
their bad marriages and
their deaths alone.
Outside was minus ten
and a wind that made you
talk to yourself.
But inside was warm,
easy and free—so that
what we felt together was
as good as anything
up on screen.

Rosie's Motel

We'd come north out of
the Chiricahua range
to stop in Willcox
for barbecue at Tony's
in the railroad car.
I said listen to that:
the flatness of afternoon
like somnolent dogs,
quiet but for overhead fans
to cushion our words.
I was thinking of selling off
and renting a room to hold
steady in till the end.
When we finished our
pulled pork on a bun
I said I gotta stop and
see somebody, you mind?
So I head over to Rosie's
thinking it's shuttered
since the pandemic and
that many years.
For service, ring the bell—
scrawled on the door.
When Rosie opened it,
ablaze in lip gloss, I said
Rosie it's me, Mr. Magoo,
come to let you know
I'm back! Not looking for
a room with a prayer
taped to the mirror, mind you,
but just to show a friend
life still is sweet.

She laughed and said,
*Mister Magoo, why you're
handsomer than ever!*
I got back in the car
and said let's go.

The Road Out

Driving somewhere south
between two states
and a restless country...
I forget. I'm moving
slow and must pull off
and stop on empty.
It takes a while

to get out of the car,
so I'll stand for a bit
in the sweetest light
before knowing what to do.
I know nothing's
for certain but that
I wish to cancel
the contract with myself
and walk, just walk
until I stop.

Acknowledgments

I'm writing this inside the cover of a book an old friend gave me over breakfast after twenty-five years apart. The clothes I wore were stained from wolfing cheeseburgers while driving single-handed down the Virgin River Gorge. She offered to launder them but I declined, choosing to keep the stains as a token. It's the life I signed up for.

I wish to thank her for starters. I won't mention her name because she already knows. She's the live-action hero the character of Lola is based on inside this thing. Had I stayed another five minutes, I'd have begun to feel the world's doing okay.

The Dips was written almost exclusively on receipts and hotel pads while I lay holed up in rm. 6303, Virgin River Hotel in Mesquite, NV. By the time I checked out it had begun breathing on its own. I returned to Tucson following a powerful storm, when I noted that nothing was prettier than a moon behind a dark cloud. It was the first time in several months I bothered to feel thankful.

So here goes. I want to thank everybody: cashiers, house maids, waitresses, especially Rosario who made it a point to seat me in her section. And all the figures that loom against a vast landscape. In Tucson, artist Jackie Goldman first used the word *dips* to mean what only she could mean. Her cover art has highlighted many of my books. Artist Sharon Butler opened her studio and allowed me to use her watercolors to accompany the poems. She worked tirelessly in making this book happen. I offer thanks to my sister, Karen, who reads every word and gets back to me, and to the members of the Hopi group who trust me with the money. Thank you, George, Tom, Ben and all the giants of the north country. And salutes to all the folks who write blurbs for my books and rave *No shit, his best yet! The sonofabitch ain't done!*

Also, heartfelt thanks to my hand therapist, Jessica Darling, for treating my carpal tunnel and finding those rubber grips to twist off stubborn bottle caps. And lastly, thank you to my tribe in Erie, Pa., for whom I will read these poems at the Poets' Warehouse this summer.

A word about the Meng-tse quote (see back cover): I came upon it years ago in Henry Miller's *From your Capricorn Friend.* It seems it was once a favorite of Hermann Hesse's, who pinned it to his door to ward off the merely curious. Then it ended up with Miller who posted it to his door while living in California. And now it's come to me at the right place and the right time. Thank you, Henry, Hermann and Meng, for saving me a seat on the midnight express. I'll just shut up now and look out the window.

about the author:

    Born in the east, he's lived in the west. One of his books was shortlisted for something. *The Dips*, his thirty-fifth offering, came at a point where little is left to say after *yes, mam* and *no thank you*, where making appointments is a bad bet, and as for keeping a promise—the last one's with yourself, and it's crucial it be kept.

about the artist:

Sharon Butler found where she belonged in life when she moved to Tucson over fifty years ago. There, in the Sonora desert, she learned how to get the right shade of pale purple by mixing and blending four different colors, as well as where to find the best Mexican food, and how to take three deep breaths and fall in love.

www.ingramcontent.com/pod-product-compliance
Lightning Source LLC
LaVergne TN
LVHW051039070526
838201LV00066B/4864